ANTIMERIDIANS

Mark Macrossan grew up in Brisbane. Previous occupations include barrister (Sydney) and film extra (London). He currently lives in Sydney.

He can be found online at www.markmacrossan.com.

Praise for ANTIMERIDIANS

'These are poems which often explore the dark side: crimes of violence, the allure of greed and power, the sufferings of loss and innocence, the chilling effects of chaos and uncertainty, yet this is tempered by a playfulness of language and a formal mastery that make the poems a pleasure to read. The charm of this book is the interplay between the *what* and the *how*, between the ability of language to explicate tragedy and drama and yet to keep true to the structures and musicality of words at their best. These poems will give you both goosebumps and delight. A fine debut collection.'

Judith Beveridge

Also by Mark Macrossan (novels)

DARK OCEANS

THE VOLCANOLOGIST

Antimeridians

POEMS 2014–2019

Mark Macrossan

ANTIMERIDIAN

First published by Antimeridian Press in 2023

This edition published in 2023 by Antimeridian Press

Copyright © Mark Macrossan 2023
www.markmacrossan.com

The moral right of the author has been asserted.

All rights reserved. This publication (or any part of it) may not be reproduced or transmitted, copied, stored, distributed or otherwise made available by any person or entity (including Google, Amazon or similar organisations), in any form (electronic, digital, optical, mechanical) or by any means (photocopying, recording, scanning or otherwise) without prior written permission from the publisher.

This is a work of fiction and any resemblance to actual persons, living or dead, is purely coincidence.

Antimeridians: Poems 2014-2019

ISBN: 9780648313687 (e-book)
ISBN: 9780648313694 (paperback)

This version: 2023-12-10

Cover design by Jonathon Eadie
www.eadie.biz

PREFACE

A meridian is a line of longitude, running north-south, from pole to pole. By contrast, a line of latitude, running east-west, is known as a 'parallel'. An *anti*meridian is the meridian on the opposite side of the world to any given meridian. Taken together, a meridian along with its antimeridian form a continuous ring of circumference around the Earth. By way of example, the antimeridian of longitude 150° East, is longitude 30° West.

The Antimeridian, with a capital A, is the meridian opposite the Prime Meridian, which runs through Greenwich in London. The Antimeridian crosses the Pacific Ocean and is used as the basis for the International Date Line. Where a map of the world is centred on the Prime Meridian – which is customary – the left and right edges of the map both represent the same line of longitude, namely the Antimeridian.

In a sense, therefore, an antimeridian represents that which exists but is hidden from any given observer's viewpoint. It's the other side of the proverbial coin; it's the edge, or the face, we don't see. It's the place that's always out of sight, but always there, balancing everything out.

Or *almost* balancing everything out.

CONTENTS

Prologue
[] (Antimeridian)   *5*

1. The Geometry Of Sails
Augmented Sonnet For A Trophy Wife   *13*
A Walk On The Glacier   *14*
Dachshund Days   *16*
Equatorial Bells   *18*
Honeymoon Man   *20*
The Murder (Of Crows) – Country Circuit   *22*
The Frozen Road   *23*
Leaves And Dust   *24*

2. Infinity Skies
I Fly   *27*
Lows And Highs   *28*
What Remains   *29*
Five To Twelve   *34*
Night Flight   *35*
Mrs Macklin's Cheese   *36*
Death Mask   *37*
The Einsteinian Qualities Of Distance   *39*

3. Arrival

Feast *43*

The Land Lies Still *45*

Rainforest Ending *46*

The News *48*

North Africa *50*

Glebe Defection *52*

Lost Explorer, Beyond Hope, Reaches Mount Oblivion *54*

A Closer Inspection 56

The Universes *58*

A note on the podor *60*

[Restaurant Scene...] *62*

Jack Of Clubs *63*

Thunderhead *64*

4. Storms

Sunrise *67*

Round Clouds *68*

The Snow That Was Falling All Day *70*

Birthnight In The Crypt *71*

The Curse *73*

The Conquistador *81*

Mason Ash *83*

Time- line *85*

The Dog On The Log *88*

The Centre Of Things *90*

5. Lines Of Longitude

By The Lee Of The Bitter Wind   *93*
The Riverbank   *99*
Goldbricker   *101*
Modern Sex   *102*
Ah Nougat   *103*
The Kiss   *104*
The Night Parrit   *106*
The Longreach Desperado   *107*
Accidental Meeting   *108*
Redux   *110*
The Unfairness Of Birds   *116*

6. A New Universe

Filaments   *121*
The Orval   *124*
Halcyone's Tears   *125*
The Blue Beauty   *128*
Aphrodite Unnosed   *129*
[] – Postscript   *131*
Littoral Motion   *132*

Previous Publications   *135*

Antimeridians

PROLOGUE

[] (Antimeridian)

Under the geometry of sails,

we arced across the globe,
tripping the spinning meridians.
Freed of today and entombed
in tomorrow, we dreamed of white-toothed
girls, and atolls, and lolling palm trees.

Riding the brimming sea, we clutched
at faithless winds that pushed and pulled us
across the map, east and west,
beyond oranges and olive groves,
towards the cloudless skies

of the blinding, mapless south.

As distance begat destiny, leathery frowns
dried to cracking in the wanton sun.
With our sharked-up barque becalmed,
dislodged from a faraway shore of memories,
the only breeze was a procession of dreams,

reflections of verdant coastlines.
Fools fooling fools: with
human flesh on the menu,
never did the remembrance
of the soot of northern towns

taste so delicious.

[]

Feel your way across infinity skies,

and swap the barrels and the starglazed nights
for a coffered treasure chest
of wildest fancy –
and tell yourself you stand a chance
of reeling in the Big Beyond.

Hook and heave away.

An abyssal nibble precedes
a fountainous leviathan splash
in reverse,
and on the deck your answer
falls, eludes you, disappears.

[]

Arrival, of a sort. Middle of the night.

The low sky had a grim taint, brushed
with the glow of southern fires. Against

the petulant curve of the shore, the slaking
waters of the bay lapped darkly.

In the crimson gloom, glued to the night-planed
surface, our slack-sailed ship held fast

in its windless cocoon. Statue-still,
a scrawny speck of a man, the lookout,

stared at the distant line of shearing flames
with wide, moon-mirror eyes, and a deep-toned

bell tolled somewhere – or so it seemed –
and when a wild dog howled to the hills,

the trees, then the cliffs, then the beach
disappeared, lost to smoke and incident,

and in this way, he – and we –
slipped quietly past an alien land.

[]

Five storms later, on a surfless coast...

Turquoise waters, shadow-hearted,
languish, and wash to a polish
the edges of the quiet shoreline.

Emerald pebbles, rounded like the bay,
set her flowing hair, ruby-red and wet;
an oyster comb tampers through the strands...

She shines. Her eyes emit a restive sea.
Her smile, her breasts, her water-folded
flesh reflect and flick away the sun.

Her scales and tail, a platform for our thoughts
but nothing more, for look too long and...
There. You see? She's gone.

[]

Time, and lines of longitude, fell away.

We came across
a sand-bottomed sanctuary,
inert beneath honey-still waters –
we were catalysed assassins
in a kindly paradise,

and despite choirs of fish
and the pageantry of rugged fruit
being the only respite from a long, thin day,
we heavy-heartedly looked to the longboats,
but then suddenly...

an invitation,

a beckoning – from beyond the beach
and past the fugitive, lava hills –
demythologizing our fantasies
and shipping us home
to a tropical judgement day at

this cleft of a place, this latent aperture,
eclipsed in the veiled interstices
of our antimeridian.

And so we delayed, and we stayed,
and we craved for nothing

but more of the same.

23° 26' 13" S   179° 59' 59" E

1. THE GEOMETRY OF SAILS

Augmented Sonnet For A Trophy Wife

Your beauty drowns the room in brilliant light,
Dazzling, like some holy aureole,
And standing there, bedecked in virgin white,
You leave us breathless, robbed of hyperbole.
O glistening object of our jealous praise,
Your polished sheen is gleaming, shiny proof
Of maintenance regimes that fill your days
And husband-wardens of your diamond youth.
Perfection needs an intervening hand
Of course. Perhaps you've had some (duller) parts
Augmented? Trimmed? Re-sculpted like Rodin?
Like touching up a fulgent work of art?
And your aurora, does it never dim?
Desire, still fiery as our nearest star?
Or are you searching for another him?
Perhaps it feels a bit like *au revoir*?
    Our ardent eyes advise a bright remark:
    Your dress is white; your shadow, widow dark.

A Walk On The Glacier

Won't someone come with me
for a blazing walk on the glacier?

And negotiate the irrational terrain, roughshod,
in the cobalt currency of our own bespoken time?

And gambol around the high seracs – those shark's-teeth
shards of ice that monument themselves to a prehistoric sky?

And cavort with glorious purpose over ragged moraines
of tilted rock? And stare in wonderment

into the smiling stretch of a crevasse –
that blue-black slit of thin that

preserves our delineated hearts and drains
the darkness from our days?

And then, you know, we could just jump in,
and plumb the undescendable depths

helpless and harnessless and full of hope,
believing in each other's reflections, what do you say.

We'd listen for cave-deep echoes of the truth
about ourselves and ignore the fact that

it's so cold down there in the faint, beryl-blue light
where the air splits and freezes

and sound dies in short, muffled breaths.
Come on, take my hand and mind your step,

our time is short, our destination
both eternal life, and death.

Dachshund Days

Derangeable bubbles
burst inside my L.A. head—
Bethany! a friend calls out
to me and I sculpt a white smile.

Bellboys and dachshunds
trot across the lobby floor,
indisposed, in the interior,
ineluctable, Bel Air air.

It's no fun for the wealthy being wealthy
you know, it's one long, losing battle
with Chance, and trying to look kind
while designing an enviable life—

The spicy scent of rhododendron,
wafting from somewhere, hints
at glacial streams and lost forests.
At some darker, muskier longitude.

O to swap this noisy palace
of chiming elevators
for a timbered Nepalese village
folded between marbled peaks.

To regift these indoor
visions of neon lives,
brittle as keenly-focused
camera shots.

What would I not trade to sing
among the sherpas and the sandalwood?
To cook! and worship gods
and mountains in the crisp, thin air—?

A commotion: the dachshunds
and the painted guests erupt, lipstuck,
excited by something only dogs
and the rich can hear.

But me, O, to inhale
the high, Himalayan breeze
and cart ice and tea
and gather wood for smoky nights...

Carpeted floors are icefalls
and mudslides, easily on, hard to get off.
Mickey Mouse is somewhere about.
O for a Tibetan suntan.

Equatorial Bells

The bleached and roofless church walls
reflect the midday glare: a ruined crown
on the jungly brow of a jagged, coral cliff.
Colonial bones. A heatworn frown.

Like the sea in a shell, you think you hear bells
resounding around the restive, turquoise bay
and clamouring through breeze-whipped palms,
reclaiming distant, irretrievable days and

chiming their appeal through the cassias
and the tamarinds, and agapanthus with their impudent heads,
and the proud old cuban trumpet trees
with their triumphant fanfare for the forgotten dead.

A bright pink shock of bougainvillea
and a blood-red poinciana tree
potently conjure a pointed thought:
might they recall the old wars of the Coral Sea?

Could they hold genetic memories of ancient storms
with their gunmetal thunderheads and gale-blasted scuds?
Of those furious cyclone days when we were all
so hot in judgement, and so ready for blood?

And then a painted parrot fractures the tranquil present
and mimics some faraway, irony peal,
and you discern an accord in the pulse of the sky
and everything tells you the bells are real.

Honeymoon Man

I saw a photograph once:
my mother's, of my father,
by the road, big smile,
honeymoon man.

Those distant da Vinci hills,
stretching away like
a memory, before
I existed,

and him, smiling
at my mother:
a slice of history,
a piece of pre-me.

A photograph marks
reflections of light,
snap-frozen and lacquered:
a footprint, a fossil in stone,

an unalterable moment
as unshiftable as Time,
essential to everything after it,
the *sine qua non*, the

without which there is nothing.

Three brief lives held
in a scintilla of light:
honeymoon man, my mother
and me.

The Murder (Of Crows) – Country Circuit*
(*an embedded haiku*)

What? When? Why?
Where? Who? How?
Oh. Or? Ahhhhh!

Winged visitors come
in their glistening black robes
with clamant questions.

Ah! Or? Oh.
How? Who? Where?
Why? When? What?!

Ahhhhhhhhhh!

---

* A *country circuit* in Australia is when judges and barristers travel to country towns 'on circuit' to hear criminal and civil cases.

The Frozen Road

A frozen road lies before me,
a hypaesthesic[1] strip of travel time –

this spasm of distance skews perspective
because I think I have you bundled in the boot.

Geysers blur the side windows and sleet
conveys the sky's disapproval.

Rocky burrs grind and scar
my forward vista, but I must hold this strictured course,

away from happy backyard days and onwards,
towards the dark-mouthed, quickening nightfall in the East.

Ah but soon the moon will rise and
oh how she will shine and turn our road

to white.

---

[1] hypaesthesia (pathology): a reduced sensibility to touch

Leaves And Dust

Crouched beneath the silty layers of
years and hidden amongst the rubble
and mulch of discarded history, noble
books in a darkened cellar, locked-in
and guarded by a flimsy key,
               let fall
leaves and dust, pages and words and
grainy photographs, evidence of lives
lived unshackled by our judgement,
only asking to be remembered by
– and not compared to – you or me.

For who are we but an extension of
a ceaseless, snaking line of stories
stretching back through scaly
        pterodactyl dreams
        to the nascent stars
        at the edge of time.

23° 26' 13" N   0° 0' 1" W

2. INFINITY SKIES

I Fly

I'm often high.
I jet my buckled line
across the sapphire sky.

I fly.

I read, I pass on by.
I pierce the clouds, I
think of things that make me smile
(and some that make me cry).

I try.

I strive to justify
my life.
I ask a lot of questions.
But all I know: I live, I love, I
die

and in the by the bye,
in all the meanwhiles,
through all the twinklings of an eye

I fly.

Lows And Highs

a drizzling flood has descended
from the sky unbidden
and settled on this cobbled land
like a sheet alighting on a bed

and now, in the squeezed, treeless streets,
gagging terracotta mud
nestles into the stacked corners
of grim de-fenced lawns as the sun

claws its way up the eastern edge of a chalk sky,
wrestles clouds off our wild damp map
and burns
a new dead drought.

What Remains

Through her he was capable of suffering, of being happy, perhaps of killing
Marcel Proust – In Search Of Lost Time

What remains?

Again the orange disk burns
darkly – almost tightly, you could say –
through the dawn torpor
and the sedimentary humidity.
Dogs and bicycles
gear up
for another show of
heat and light,
and smells, crushed through
with their own ripeness,
oil the parts for the sake
of the whole.

And the whole
jigsawed biosphere,
here,
welcomes me
and the rest of hell,
welcomes the shocked
and the free,

welcomes the staring red emperors,
and the severed coconuts,
welcomes the corpse-like durian,
and all the while the purging, post meridiem
storm is still a forecast,
still a dream.

Dawn is
the darkest time.

*

What remains of my life

now that I've lost her?
Somewhere east of Istanbul.
The white-tipped Caucasus, the Karakum
sands. She's out there, somewhere,
but she's dead, you see.
Maybe not to the world
(I wouldn't know),
but she's dead to me.

Was our crime
too much for her?
Or did she miss them,

the dead-them
more than the living-me?

*

What remains of the bodies?

A typhoon is churning
somewhere over the horizon,
flinging clouds and
clawing at the ocean,
sucking up water and fish,
but not, regrettably,
sucking up me.

The South China Sea
is the nightmare;
the dream is
that kitchen floor in Victoria,
Virginia, USA, with its blooming
ruby pool.

'Remains? What remains?'
One with thirty-two stab wounds.
'But how is that possible, officer?',
'Her parents, they were rich, sure,
but they had no enemies...'

*

Whatever remains is the truth,

once you take away the impossible,
so says Sir Arthur Conan Doyle.
And so, here? What remains here?

Here, where all the escapees
from the bright world go.
Where day is night,
and life is death.

*

What remains to be said

is absolutely nothing at all
(except that *murder*
is ugly in American,
in any accent but Scottish, I guess).

*

What remains

after all those disapproving looks?
Cause and effect.
What did they expect.

Five To Twelve

You never hear the church bells
chime their midday celebration
when it's always five to twelve
and all the clocks have rusted to a stop.

Nevermore will he bring that loyal kettle to the boil
or allow the tea its perfect time to draw,
or deal out little wisdoms like Plato's croupier
or recommend a village or a cheese.

Our lives will never be different again,
from now to eternity nothing will change:
He left us in the morning a little after tea
and the pot will be drawing evermore for me.

Night Flight

Spread out like a midnight flood
the cold and pitiless expanse of ocean
smothers the night-time earth below.

An oily void unkissed by moonlight
a dark which only high and distant stars defy
while feckless clouds have fled on shifty winds.

I scratch my ear and rest my head against the plastic pane
know nothing about vectors or throttles or flaps
but puzzle about the heading and the destination

and where we are on the map if we haven't flown off it.
And I wonder if we will ever be free of
this endless, faceless, ink-black sea.

Mrs Macklin's Cheese

Mrs Macklin serves the cheese,
while her husband's shadow shuffles
thinly by along the corridor behind her...

Mrs Macklin loved her daily cheeses,
and her husband did so equally,
(in the days when he still ate).

Mrs Macklin liked them creamy,
liked them piquant,
liked them blue and daring
– so did Mrs Macklin's husband (when he ate).

Gruyere, Comté, Gorgonzola,
Camembert and Pecorino
Brie, Manchego, Vacherin,

Mrs Macklin's cheeses priced
themselves within her limits
unlike business class or opera nights...

She cuts a slice of Wensleydale
and eats it with a fig
as her husband, in the background, slips away.

Death Mask

You what? she says.

Panic point.
Thudding.
Clotted words
hitting a fan.

You what? she screams.

The friable sky
incandesces
and crackles.
Trees smoulder,
walls of water crash
through bamboo-stilted
villages. Dogs cringe and flee.
The sun's long gone and the moon hides.

Air-raid sirens wail as I
dive into the mudbrown
zigzaggèd trench
and bury my face
in a glutinous
death mask.

Worms shift away,
oozing embarrassment.
You what? they say.

The Einsteinian Qualities Of Distance
(*a sestina*)

It seems only yesterday a disorienting sense
of unease, and the shrinking autumn sun,
and the scattering leaves of the plane
trees all told me it was time
to escape these iron-born, sky-wrapping clouds,
and drive, or fly, or take a (now impossible) train

journey to you. For years I'd needed to train
myself to deal with the singularity of your absence,
with the state of living under different clouds,
in a different city to you, my old, only son
– with having to face these longitudes and time
zone discrepancies – and not just jump on a plane,

and land on your doorstep. The dry, boundless plain
that stretches between us, spanned only by dead train
lines and gouged-out roads and sheep, stretches Time
somehow, beyond borders or meridians, or a sense
of reality, and is measured in megalitres of sun,
wingbeats of crows, claps of thunder, and clouds

– a barrier as tangible and solid as brick. It clouds
our thinking, this quantity of distance that only a plane

can take on (devouring the miles while it races the sun).
Walking's too slow (Life's too short) and you hit rain
squalls and rockfalls in four-wheel-drives. In a sense,
they're partners in crime: fat Distance and hungry Time.

But everything had changed this time.
My room was a prison I couldn't leave. Clouds
of memories cast shadows of doubt and my sense
of gravity failed me. My eyes lied. A passing plane
flew tail-first across the sky. A passing train
of thought reified, opalescent in the west-rising sun.

And now nothing remains, including you, my son,
or not for me. I've crossed a line in Time
that no one recrosses. The curtains of distant rain
always stay away, and their dark, mothering clouds
forever float far beyond my windowpane, in plain
sight but unknowable in this, my eternal loss of essence.

I have a sense of it now: the relativity of Time
clouds the amplitudes of Distance on our brief train
journey across the endless plain and on, into the sun.

0° 0' 1" N   90° 0' 0" E

3. ARRIVAL

Feast

Sweet smells well up
from a grille in the ground.
Duck fat crackles
somewhere, in a pan.
She's cooking my life
into a confit of fragrant
endings.

Because somewhere down there,
beyond the stairs,
the napkins and knives
are ready. Just-opened wine
burbles free.
Pepper and cinnamon,
salted cod.
Gold meringue and sweetened lies.
Luscious hills, ripe cathedrals,
bite-sized chunks of books,
desires,
dripping dancers,
perfect answers,
marinated snow,
and fog.

She throws it in and out
it comes, my life complete, and all she says is
Eat! my sweet
Eat!

The Land Lies Still

The land lies still and heavy.
Waiting for something to happen.
Waiting for rupture,

for cataclysm, for a tearing
upheaval, a ripping of day into night,
waiting for change.

The morphine air hangs gravid and birdless –
the only proof of the existence of time
is the pressing pulses of the cicadas
and the inching of the shadows.

In lumbering partnership with that timbal trill,
the deaf heat shudders through faded leaves
of battered trees. The old creek bed

settles, with infinite patience. A Mona Lisa smile
etched in its canyoned courses. Content enough,
it would seem, for now,
to be dry.

Rainforest Ending

The footprints end
where the forest begins.

Cat's claw creeper vines
hang
like empty nooses and
the dank darkness weighs down
the disappearing light.
The black's what seeps
into your head now,
your head
but not your memory,
of which there's nothing left
but shoe impressions.

You hear an animal, a bird,
like a baby's cry –
or a scream –
and pools of water –
or blood – squelch and rise
around your printless feet.

Night falls like a slab of stone
and left is right, and up is down.

And then, before your useless eyes
somewhere
a metal sound
which is when you know
she'll never be seen again.

Which is when you wonder
who'll wonder if you will.

The News

And now the news.
Bonsoir à tous
and welcome all to
wreckage and the magnitude
of slaughtered
sheep
and people, damage still to be assessed.

The tests require
expect no sleep
contamination is extensive.

Overwhelming devastation
first we have to warn you:
viewers may find scenes upsetting
and the scale of the disaster
should they not succeed in
-vestigations into
estimations based on
catastrophic
computations
helpless children on the
ground the picture's bleak
and news is yet to reach

all dead and washed up on the beach.

The earthquake toll
and little hope for most
the mud
the flood
the village washed away.
And now to sport.

Recapping
bleeding
we look forward to your
hope you have a lovely evening.

North Africa

Pigeons scuttling in gutters
over arched windows with
black gaping holes
– open mouths
exhaling clouds of spiced
Tunisian smoke.

Plated, oblivious voices spilling
from the accessory darkness
within.

The bare concrete stairwell
belies an untidy tragedy:
door ajar, persian carpet
crumpled, candelabras
overturned. An oasis
of pleasure violated.
A super-Saharan getaway
cut short. No way
to treat a lady,
all this blood and lapis lazuli,
and her American friend, as well,
both dead – just bodies on
my unmade bed.

The birds and smoke and voices
accuse me every humid second
that pounds between now
and a desperate, doorless future.

Glebe Defection

sensorily deprived
in a crumbling
terrace
bereft
of reason

creeper vines
piercing
her
brain

the tenuousness
of his love
was enough
to frack
their soft foundations
like the knotted roots
of the neighbour's fig tree

seeking distance always reaching...

she broke free in summer
sprinting through a damning rain
and a post-monsoonal glare

towards another life
a clipped new jungle
and autumn people who said they cared

Lost Explorer, Beyond Hope, Reaches Mount Oblivion

Jagged flakes of tossed-out lava
litter the slope like broken glass,
sulphurous smoke smears the sky.

A vista as parched as my ash-
filled throat. Breathing
restricted to gasps now.

Final entry. The verdant,
thronging inland sea, if it exists,
does not exist for me. And yet

this waterless, birdless, lifeless
view includes a sea of sorts
(a cruel joke): a shining lake

of magma. Liquid rock, boiling
and flipping, cracking, mocking,
quencher of nothing but a thirst for death,

incandescent manhole
to the centre of the earth,
coruscating porthole

to the limits of the imagination.
Am just a headlong dive away
from molten consummation.

A Closer Inspection

A closer inspection of a once-loved speckled-oak desk revealed, attached to what looked like a splintery drawer, a blackened iron handle, which fell off when I touched it. And when I took to the desk with a rusty hammer, levering my way through years of neglect, the bottom of the drawer fell out and hundreds of baby spiders scattered across the floor, fleeing, their tiny black bodies a blur of disparate, disappearing full stops. . .

After the sudden diaspora, a disintegrating pile of papers was all that remained. I lay on the dusty floor and blew. The uppermost leaf lifted and floated like a genie's carpet and words, like the spiders, were suddenly everywhere. Filling the air like love. . .

Words and letters, up my nose and in my clothes, hammering down like purposeful rain on a loving, world-weary roof of tin, then burrowing in, embedding themselves in my head, in my brain...

I tried to get them out, those words. For years I did my best but three remain. The first is 'I', the third is 'you'. Yet no amount of love or money will reveal the identity of word number two.

The Universes

The silkworm wakes, all spun inside an airless vault,
as the red-faced baby shakes and screams
for something richer beyond its grasp;
the frightened woman argues with the air
as she stands atremble at the open window
with its view of leafless trees and foggy smoke;
and beneath a set of stony peaks I lose my feet
in shifting granite scree,
corkscrew round and fall
and as I do, I look to the abyss
beneath. And there they are,
the final pages of my life,
just falling rocks and gravity
until
her grasping hand holds fast to mine,
stretching miles
and bridging time before
I'm standing at the open window
with its view of emerald trees
bestowing shade and growing skywards out of cracked cement;
the standing woman smiling as the quiet baby sleeps;
the moth emerging, ripping silk with boundless confidence.

A note on the podor

A podor is a particular poetic form (making its debut here, in this collection).

The name is a corruption of the French, *pot d'or* (pot of gold).

A podor is made up of five quatrains, each with an *ABAB* pattern of end rhymes (or near-rhymes) and a regular metre, usually tetrameter. All of the lines in the final stanza are repeated lines (exact replicas, aside from punctuation), with one line taken from each of the previous four stanzas. The idea is that the meaning of the repeated lines in the final stanza changes (due to enjambment, punctuation shifts, and each line's relationship to the lines around it), and that the final stanza provides an answer to a question collectively posed by the previous four stanzas.

The final stanza becomes, therefore, the pot of gold.

That's the theory at least. The following two poems in this collection, *[Restaurant Scene...]* and *Jack Of Clubs*, are evidence of attempts to put this theory into practice.

In the third poem, *Thunderhead*, the final stanza is made up of words and phrases, rather than whole lines, taken from the previous stanzas (and they are taken haphazardly, as opposed to from one line from each stanza), and that poem might therefore be more accurately described as a quasi-podor.

[Restaurant Scene...]
(*a podor*)

When she appears it's like sunrise:
he dreams she's over near the door.
She greets him with her wild, brown eyes.
Just like she used to do, before...

His company's an empty chair.
It would have once been Genevieve.
They used to come here every year...
But now she's living overseas.

Across the crowded room he stares
and sips his wine and brings to mind
the day she left him, the despair...
The end of two lives intertwined.

Avoiding looks from laughing eyes
he contemplates the *plat du jour*.
But through the clattering of knives
he hears the yawning of the door...

Across the crowded room he stares.
Avoiding looks from laughing eyes.
His company's an empty chair
when she appears. It's like sunrise.

Jack Of Clubs

(*a podor*)

The prying moonlight, stained maroon,
bleeds through angled wooden blinds.
You make out a naked girl in the gloom,
and the blood, and take notes of the scene of the crime.

The picture's plain enough. Though under
the dancer's hand you see a card:
a knave, like the thug who killed her, and clubs,
both his modus, and the dives where she danced.

The battered corpse can't tell you who
the perpetrator of this violence
is. You just ask the Easter moon
instead, but all you hear is silence.

But wait. A bloody thumbprint perhaps?
On the card? Then a noise makes you turn your head to
your right. Pocket the Jack of Clubs
you think (but why?), and you bolt from the bedroom.

The picture's plain enough though, under
the prying moonlight: stained maroon,
your right pocket. The Jack of Clubs
is you. Just ask the Easter moon.

Thunderhead

(*a podor*)

Captain's log, year of the Lord eighteen eighty-four:
waterlogged, blood-soaked, baked in the sun.
Gone are the gales, the blue world's restored,
but it's after the tempest that the worst always comes.

After port master's whistle and the vanishing crowds,
after breeze-puffed sails chased down a dark evening,
the red morning pinned us a note in the clouds,
and foreboding descended, like salt on the rigging.

Embodying our fears, a thunderhead loomed:
its scribbles in lightning are futures redrawn;
with these gunmetal sentinels, these portenders of doom,
the veneer of civilization is gone.

All four of us emerged from the storm in a lifeboat;
in the interminable calm, we all dreamed of home...
and of one thing in particular: what we craved most
was reprieve from the *hunger* – anything, bones...

Embodying the worst that descended was when
all three of us, blood-soaked, our hunger redrawn,
were discovered, adrift and baked in the sun,
the veneer of civilization gone.

0°0' 1" S   90°0' 0" W

4. STORMS

Sunrise

The pomegranate seeds,
the coconut husks, the gnawed-
out melon, all evidence that they were near.
That they were here.

Dawn stings the fleeing, dying night, while trees
stretch away as far as sight. Distance,
my erstwhile friend, wears me down and
throws its tangents over me like a net.

Wheeling birds, my white
lieutenants, my loud, reliable scouts,
screech ancient warnings. Time
washes away like sodden debris
down a stream.

And something clogs.

When the shot rang out, the ball of lead
crashed through ferns, left me dead.

Round Clouds

One holds an
Obdurate fear
Of round clouds.

Or should hold one.

Ordinary storms roll on past
Opening the odd umbrella – they're
Over before you know it. Those with ominous,
Oval undersides, though, orchestrate a greater mayhem.

Out our southern window, one
Occasionally spots, from October
On, a horizonal blot, a mottled blob, an
Overhung mammatocumulus cloud formation
On the hop, bulbous pouches pointing downwards, like an
Onslaught of oversized bosoms, or bottoms, or a doom-bound multitude

Of atom bombs. Beware. Those lowering,
Opalescent pillows of the apocalypse hold an
Odious load: a billowing cargo of pandemonium, an
Odium of ogres in loathful oratorio. Both omnipotent and
Overblown, those dark-hearted Othellos of the troposphere, those
Overhead oligopolists, those ozoned oligarchs of chaos, come weaponed with

Omnivorous tornadoes and cannonball hailstones, with
Obliterations of rain and torrents of
Ordeal. So when that blue,
Overhead vault turns
Overcast and grey,

One always observes the golden rule: if it's r-
Ound, go to ground.
Or else. OK?

The Snow That Was Falling All Day
(*a villanelle*)

And the snow had been falling all day
at Moscow airport. There was a sense
of a tragedy heading their way.

And the air had been heavy and grey.
The pilot though, had not been concerned
that the snow had been falling all day.

And conditions were fair. No delays,
runways clear, there was nothing to warn
of a tragedy heading their way.

And the only unease was conveyed
by a deep-seated fear at the sight
of the snow that was falling all day.

And until the lone snowplough had strayed
onto the tarmac, there was no hint
of a tragedy heading their way...

And then impact. And nothing remained
but the plough, and the necklace of fires,
and the snow that was falling all day
before tragedy headed their way.

Birthnight In The Crypt

It's nothing more than scripture,
only fallow vellum leaves,
just dirt and dust and air.

    π

There's a candle guttering in the crypt.
Mars has passed the ascending node,
the moon's flung far beneath.

These knotted orbits
play out against a settling
of the darkness:

as the wealthy and the hoodwinked
ease to sleep, and forests
sigh away the leaving of the day,

as night-drenched ditch-diggers,
lugging tools, pick their way
along a shifting path of sludge,

beneath them all, in the hypogean
gloom of this sunken, flickering cavity,
a voice, torn from an echo, is stifled to extinction.

       π

Because it's only ever scripture.
Just fallow, vellum leaves.
Just dirt, and dust, and air.

       π

It's the birthday of some dead king, and he
(or what's left of him), with choking,
plaintive sobs is digging – digging down –

through the broken bones and the petrifying earth
in his search for eternal validation,
for a collective memory lost

to the ravages of decay – to the relentless rain
and the burdened winds, to the change-charged air
– and now mixed in with the deep, blood-brown

of burial clay.

The Curse

Omnia mutantur, nos et mutamur in illis

A curse settles over the city
like invisible drizzle. Or ash.
The wind changes, and dies down,

and all movement slows to a fugitive rest.
Roger Bird, 31, of Lakehurst, lowers
and holds his shaking hand.

Anne O'Sullivan, 55, of East Meade,
discovers she's holding her breath.
Jess Ferris, 22, of Highwall, steers his car

through a fence and waits, as Blake Johnson,
41, of Mayfield, while changing, forgets
how to tie his tie. A tightness and

an irritating tickle in her throat bothers
Amber Rundle, 9, of the outer
suburb of Foresthide...

The curse pools
and seeps into cracks
in the pavement with

the carelessness of killers.
Unseeable layers inch down
on windscreens and awnings

and the freshly-turned earth of building sites.
Coal-flecked clouds deform and unravel.
The russet-red sun flickers wanly.

At the airport, an arctic, liquid fog
greets brittle passengers – no one
speaks in Departures and no one

arrives in Arrivals. And all the while,
quiet as midnight, the curse cakes and
hardens to an impervious patina.

All movement slows. The wind dies
down. Invisible ash drifts and loops
and settles in piles on the cold, cold ground.

*

There's a wrinkle in the sky, a change
of light, and I feel a little strange. As if
a transmigrated soul has somehow
made its way inside. As if everything

I ever learned was learned to kill
the time. There's something foreign,
something pulsing, in the air.
Eighteen people died today in

my suburb alone – died alone –
and everyone's afraid. Streetlights fail
and nothing prospers, not even bad
intentions. Thieves and bankers

head for work and lose
their way. Supermarkets
close and everybody's changing
their religion, even atheists.

As I fly the crack between despair
and hope, my shadow adumbrates
a fickle vision of a future. I live
– I mean survive – on petrol,

fries and coca-cola
as the long, black
hole slowly
angles in.

*

What's left of the hunter's moon will be your
  cursory guide
in the day-for-night crepuscule. The white sands of
  the beach stand out

against the black of the ocean beyond. Your dress is
  torn, you rest
on a rock, accepting the brief respite from the
  pursuit. Waves pound

the distant reef, deep in the night in front of your
  eyes. But no rest is true, no
sleep is sound anymore, not for you, not for any of
  you. Behind you,

coming from the jungle road that stitches the low,
  dark hill, the sound of
slipping gravel curdles through the broken trees.

You turn to face it, wide eyes
reflecting the dead light.

It's that man, your friend, arriving, grasping
like the newly-blind, swatting the thick night air.

He's changed. But not his torn blue suit, his clay-
 caked shoes or his wild,
sodden hair. And then you catch that sound again:
 a fusillade of muffled,

choking peals, pitched and panted, with the dogged
 proximity of tinnitus.
You point towards a rocky promontory a kilometre
 away at least.

Our only hope, you hear yourself say. You cannot
 see it but you know
it's there (you abandoned doubt and married belief
 a myriad slivered

moons ago). You bound, alone, along the beach, or
 try to, through
the uncooperative sand, as white lines of small
 waves abruptly appear

in the darkness just when you forget them, scaring
 you, before fading
away again and dissipating in the shifting shallows.
 The only sounds:

the lapping water, your footfalls, your clutching,
  fitful breathing. The sounds
of failure and loss.

*

A curse has made our city
its home, its DNA once stored,
now thawed and folding, blending

with our own. It happened when
the wind dropped. And now the slippery
feel of innovation coats the withered

leaf within: a transfigured photosynthesis
pervades. An automatic upgrade. The smell
of ceaseless variation taints the air.

Because it was always there,
dug well in, with a patience
no one noticed, waiting for

the blossoming.
The low-pitched hum
of alteration echoes

through the empty sky,
through the childless
parks, the carless streets,

the treeless,
dogless, dead
backyards.

The only crop is mould – the yeast
we're left to eat, the bitter taste
of transformation.

Everyone's a doppelgänger
now, we're *vardogers*,
appearing before we arrive, and

leaving with the certainty
of killers. No books or news,
just déjà vu, and everywhere

the will o' the wisp, the *irrbloss*,
the pinpoints of light on sunken
moors, and the *huldra*,

with their hollow backs, and their crooked
look of transmutation.

Comfortless *mylings* roam

the streets, ghosts of children
seeking burials, seeking peace.
And as the celestial bodies

emblazoned across the ecliptic plane
churn out their endless,
restless rhythm,

we metamorphose,
gradually, and limb by limb,
we turn ourselves to stone.

*

All movement slows.
The wind dies down.
Invisible ash drifts and

loops, until there is,
at last,
no soul around.

Omnia mutantur, nos et mutamur in illis – 'All things are changing, and we are changing with them'

The Conquistador

I

Pierced and pummelled and browned,
he plummeted through the racking undergrowth,
condemned by ghosts of painted cannibals
hanging like fruit in the canopy above,

while the snow-tipped peaks in the brittle distance
glinted askew in the midday sun
like swords of gods demanding justice,
or the teeth of the beast this land had become.

The tumbledown farmhouse near Seville
was now just a dream, a silent world away
from this heat and this sweat
and the bitter knives only half a day behind him,

because his blood will be theirs.
He'd had his share,
of lives (but not gold), and soon his god
would judge him, boots and skulls and all.

II

Baltasar lay
on the jungle floor
with the ants.

Dreamlessly.

Without thoughts of harvests,
or Luisa, or the echo
of children's laughter,

or the gold that he sought, or
the blood that he spread, or
the girls that he carried to his bed

crying,
light as leaves,

or the men that he dared
to follow him
beyond the white volcanoes.

Mason Ash

The shout went out
that he had felt his way
to over-friendliness
shall we say
        with two young girls.

Evie and Maya were
currawonging their way across
the neighbourhood one sunny
afternoon among the plane trees
        and the tall school boys.

Along with the myna birds
they shrieked and shrilled
their time away and chanced
upon a man called Mason Ash
        who sharpened knives for cash.

A bright and chirpy conversation
turned to black when Evie implied
that Mason had eyed her up
the other day when she was
        swimming in the local pool.

Mason waved them off
like pesky flies
and never expected Detective
McBride to pay a house call
        later on that cloud-filled eve.

'You sharpen knives and
now you're trying your hand
at something softer' taunted
the copper who clocked his suspect's
        gaunt and guilty-looking face.

'I never did' was Mason's
plain defence but in comparison
though true it paled beside
the children's wicked tale
        of colourfully despicable events.

The truth and nothing but

the man who lived in Strathfield
with his sadly-smiling mother now
listens in his cell to the concrete echoes
of his thoughts warding off the words
        the crowds outside the courthouse yelled:

Mason Ash will rot in hell !!

Time- line

Clocks   tick
Time   slips

Sun-   rise
Pink   sky

Rain   falls
Bird-   calls

Seas   lap
ice-   caps

Up-   turn
Banks   earn

Clocks   slip
Time   sticks

Sun   fries
Creeks   dry

Ash   palls
Birds   fall

Ice caps
col- lapse

Tide turns
Banks burn

Crime sprees
Dead seas

Whales float
like boats

Drums roll
Bells toll

Heads roll
Death toll

Fault line
Bad sign

Floor shakes
Glass breaks

Ground dips
Fields   flip

Hills   glow
Rocks flow

No   air
No   prayer

No   dice
Good- night

Earth rends
Men end

No   sense
No   hence

No   when
but then.

The Dog On The Log
(*a pantoum*)

It was *him*. I saw him again.
The dog on the log.
I was just out for a nonchalant walk
in the fog. He looked like a frog,

the dog on the log,
just crouching in silence, ready to pounce.
In the fog he looked like a frog
or rather a rat.

Just crouching in silence, ready to pounce,
he sat like a cat with his eye on a bird.
Or rather a rat
lost in its thoughts.

He sat like a cat with his eye on a bird
unaware of the danger and
lost in its thoughts,
all plump and ready for eating.

Unaware of the danger and
whistling softly, I edged closer,
all plump and ready for eating.
The dog opened wide and showed me his teeth.

Whistling softly I edged closer
still, dreaming of crispy-skin chicken, when
the dog opened wide and showed me his teeth
and roared like a lion.

Still dreaming of crispy-skin chicken when
I should have been more alert, I screamed
and roared like a lion,
running like buggery for the nearest tree.

I should have been more alert. I screamed
Call in the air force! before the little bastard,
running like buggery for the nearest tree,
disappeared from view.

*Call in the air force before the little bastard
kills someone!* I yelled to no avail, and
disappeared from view,
hoping I'd *never* see that dog on a log...

But I did. It was him. I saw him again.

The Centre Of Things

The headlong sea churned
with loss and loneliness
– as it so often does, to her, it seems –
the night the crabs came in.

The purple, moonless sky
was thickening in its own invisible light,
the fishless shallows
rippling with secret purpose,

and with eyes saucered wide,
she was listening to the ceiling cracks,
and the sound of corduroy swells
crumpling on a distant reef

when suddenly, softly, the sea,
as it always did, drew the crabs
and the windy-haired girl who lived on her own,
and the lonely light of the hidden moon

back to the centre of things.

66° 33' 47" S   0° 0' 0" E

5. LINES OF LONGITUDE

By The Lee Of The Bitter Wind

['By the lee': (*Naut.*) so that the wind is blowing on the wrong side of the sail]

Behold the brutal face

Beyond the brimming
spindrift and the sheer gaol-high bluffs
with their wave-beaten
hooves
of vulcan rock and rough
and across the long distempered sea
a low-born murmur of thunder shudders
over hordes of lunging
whitecaps
those bleak devotees of tumult
and calamity

A volcano laboured for a million years
just for him
blasting and carving this ragged
slab of basalt

this wind-worn ruin
and even
the gannet the plover and those other
lovers of the foaming seas have no
extended business here
just tempests and sharks and
desperate buccaneers

A scored peak overtowers the spot
where he sits
staring out over oblivious tides
to the careless horizon
a fresh point of view
a place
to slip his briny chains and
riding flying thoughts escape
this mouldy limbo
this soulless bond between his turbid past
and whatever lies beyond

Mapwise everything lies beyond

The prime meridian
europe

savage coasts and dark continents
all visited by the same hard-
boiled emissary
the sun
time-bound reminder
that his purpose now is to watch the sky
as the billowing clouds
of chance
sail by

For a man with no home
there's no word for return

All the king's troops couldn't hold him
were his destiny not this outrage
this remotest of rocks
this eternal dismastment where
torment comes dressed in english names
such as *longwood* and *hudson lowe*
and *the honourable east india co*
and where the chinese
and the lascars and all of the slaves
are all of them ghosts
just like the waves

For in the crack between two worlds
dreams are real and the rest is air

His entourage and other people
exist in bubbles of their own

---

no more talk and no more coffee

---

barren times yield lean choices
shame-soaked abdication or a
musket ball in the head? is it
better to be barely alive? or dead?

---

how is a course of action wrong?
what is the definition of right?

---

just france
the army
josephine

(no more coffee
no more talk)

---

europe will thrive without him both
better for him and worse for him so
where was the error? waterloo was
no great loss (fortune won the day)

---

but france?
the army?

---

josephine?

---

how can you live without love?

---

in a storm-torn pavilion
or the shadow of *notre
dame* it's all the same

So you train your grey eyes seaward until
you glide like an albatross
across the speckled distance
past africa
past the sun
past history
and on into the night

and there you will lie with the thunder
with your soul undimmed
and there you will lie
in the lee of fate's bitter wind

And they'll say you were great
oh they'll say you were great

The Riverbank

The optimism of the day
gives way to the night's
dark predictions,
the paisley shades of distant skies
to midnight's lowering cloak of smog,
choked with smells of dog and burning.

Fruit bats smack the air
and moonlit waters shimmer
and scatter after vanishing boats;
the mangroves quicken
with mosquitoes and mudskippers,
with murmur and gurgle and gloat.

Her Gallic accent always attracted
the best of the beasts and the worst
– like a light trap – but bold olive skin
and a pertinent backpack were no match
for the ruin sprung forth after dusk
by the gorged, primordial riverbank.

Because it all comes out at night:
the losses, the fears, the rawboned years,
the grief, the latitudinal dreams,

the barbarous designs of shrunken
minds, the glutted lies, the times when
nothing was ever what it seemed.

And nothing ever is. Twigs crack. Twist
your back. Fight it like a heart
attack. Feel the tightened grip of mudded
limbs. Behold a dogged horror germinate
in oil-black silt. Judder to surrender,
succumbing to the pitched and lumpen night.

Pale skin glows by the water's edge.
Who knows the words of the stunted prayer
that lost its meaning in that mortal sludge.
Lost its sunken voice in the strait-laced
lapping of the heedless ripples, the river's
cast-offs, of which this body, now, is one.

Goldbricker

Bring me a barrow of golden ingots:
we'll build us a shining tower
that'll climb all the way to the tips of the clouds
and make all our enemies glower.

Bring me a shower of ruby red kisses:
we'll build us a wonderful life
we'll travel the world and drink the best wines
and do it as husband and wife.

Bring me your money, every last cent.[1] [2] [3]

---

[1] as prices these days tend to burgeon

[2] even Love's going to cost you an arm and a leg

[3] not to mention the fees of the surgeon

Modern Sex

Sun on glass, and concrete walls,
tied up, tongue-tired, tease me more.

Penthouse bought for sixteen million,
shows us all her full Brazilian.

Haute couture and cutting edge,
three's a crowd on double beds.

Rooftop looks like Shangri-La,
playing her like a sweet guitar.

Hipsters, pop stars, adulation,
foreplay without copulation.

iPods, iPads, iPhones humming,
goings-on and second comings.

Choking smog and traffic snarl,
dental dams and *hi, I'm Carl.*

Ah Nougat

Ah nougat,
I miss her.

I miss her lovely,
I miss her chewy,
I miss her nutty.

I miss her naughty!

I miss her tricky, her trickier,
I miss her sweet, her sweeter,
I miss her sweetest of all.

Ah nougat!
I miss her lovely.

The Kiss

No. Not him.
Don't hand me over.

Swap places. Why
don't *you* be the one

to cringe at the leathery hand
infecting *your* virginal skin.

To smell that rank horse breath,
that booze factory. Hell's guts.

To silently scream *shark attack*
as his sandpaper cheek rushes in.

To witness those thin corruptible lips
slobbering like a wide-eyed Doberman...

Unhandle me.
Unkiss me...

But I am tainted, doomed,
cursed and deformed. I am ruined.

I was assaulted by the Prime Minister last Thursday.
Me, who hasn't even had his first birthday.

The Night Parrit

The night parrit is a butifal burd.
He puffs himself up like a marcho nerd.
And when his excighted he bownses arownd
and bangs his nerdie head on the grownd.
Evryone loves the night parrit.

Pleas god save him from becumming extinct.
Long life and branes are no dowt linked.
And that's why I worry abowt my fethry frend,
his not the smartest tool in the shed.
And who cudnt love the night parrit.

Pleas god save this onederful thickhead
and keep him safe from stupud dickheads.
But just in case, ill take one home.
And stuff him and swop him with the garden nome.
Then evryone can see the night parrit.

Coz who wudnt love the night parrit?

The Longreach Desperado
for Bill Newton 1929-2014

You're out there, at large, in the fenceless lands,
from the banks of the Barcoo to the Broadbeach sands,
and you're up to no good, or that's what they say –
but if that's what no good is, give me bad any day.

You're the highway bandit who holds up no coaches,
the desperado who's honest and appears on no posters.
You're the black-flagged pirate who chases no ships:
your cutlass is kindness, your guns are your quips.

You're the towering rogue wave that doesn't break.
You're the rattling tremor that's never a quake.
You're the tropical cyclone that steers a wide berth.
You're that red-flaming rock that just missed the earth.

You're a cheeky smile pretending to sin.
You're the off-limits club we all want to be in.
You're the mug lair who's not one, who's just acting it out.
You're a lover of freedom, the last knockabout.

And at night in the outback when it's cold and it's clear
and the stars are like torches, blazing and near,
the brightest one winking is no simple star:
it's you, showing us the good that you are.

Accidental Meeting

Coincidental meetings
on light-starved streets
bespeak unpleasant meanings.

Twilight apparition
summoned from the shadows,
old friend, ex-friend, someone else's girlfriend...

I hadn't seen Lena
in eight long years
and now she'd grown a bigger set of ears.

*I've heard you're mixing
with some pricks who
fix flash cars, mate. Care to comment?*

Lena's icy-blue stare stung
my eyes and, needling in,
took a biopsy of my vinoed brain.

Is that the time? I said, *I gotta
fly. You're looking great!
It looks like rain.*

Miss you Rob, so
text me, eh?
We should do a drink one day.

A drink with her?
How about next hellsday.
But why did that feel like today?

As she turned to go
rejoining the shadows
her parting remark:

And by the way. Those cars
of yours are happenings
waiting for accidents.

Three days later, driving home,
spotting wreckage burnt and shoddy,
Sergeant Brody found my body.

Redux

1. A Geological History

Once, there were no rivers,
there were no glistening limestone peaks,
no broken, grandiloquent canyons,
no snowbound forests of pine.

Before thundering gorges and delta-lands,
before oceans and shimmering sea-ice,
before scimitar beaches and fat summer clouds,
there was faulting and folding, and noise.

There was hope.

2. The Rise Of Man

It slowly arose
from the quieted earth,
sludge dropping in clumps
on the sodden ground,
soil and weeds upheaved
and cloddishly dumped down.

It stretched and rasped,
appendages and pinions and
granite limbs cracking to life,
the pale moon a witness
as it rose and stood,
clenched and heartless, before

its stone eyes opened.

3. Ellipsis

Everything comes from moments.
From the first explosion.
From the first orgasm.
From the first idea.

If you wait long enough
all moments will happen.
There's a queue.
Make sure you're in it.

From the first thrown stone.
From the first rocket to the moon.

From lust and curiosity.
From love.

4. The Arch

(The Roman arch, like love, is
always striving for perfection,
always desperately trying
to avoid falling inwards.)

5. The Downfall Of Western Civilization

There's a word, or a phrase, that's kind of like
eating away at our lives, it's chewing our conversations

like a virus or a cow,
kind of munching like

an unstoppable force.
Like a cancer. Like

how can you talk of weapons of mass destruction
when you're like firing them out of your mouth?

6. The Coming

The horizon wrinkles and darkens.
The stillness of distant geometry
awakens.

All falls to silence.

A scarlet morning, a storm warning,
a four-dimensional night leaks
into the day, congeals in the sky.

It looks like mud.

7. Afternoons, After The Apocalypse

Schisms and cataclysms,
another bad afternoon.
It's still tea at 3, though,
for just the two of us,
no bookings required.

All forms of transport are out of reach.
Who would believe it? Would have foreseen it?

We're stuck here, lifewrecked
on a beach. Or is it a peach? Or a pear?
Or a pair of fools, because breathable air

is what's missing. And chirpy conversation.
So we just lie here, conscious (just),
panting in the littoral zone,
praying for God
but wishing for home.

Wishing it would come,
wishing we could go.

8. Introspection

(Always resort to resorts
I always say, when your
days go astray.)
Killing my cigarette
in its *See You In Hell* ashtray
I make a decision.

When I die (which will be soon)
I'll have them freeze my brain,
I'll sit out the intervening dark ages
      in a jar.

Yes, in a jar! And return
refreshed and looking for love.

O chop off my head and save the best for last!

I'll live a cloistered life:
lots of books, indoor fun
      (if you know what I mean!),
maybe take in a movie.
No harm indulging in a little
self-reflection now and then.

No harm in a bit of introspection.
I'll keep to myself and dine alone.
No harm in being on the shelf,
      so to speak.
           No harm in a spot of
      navel-gazing.

Life in a jar, it's not everyone's
      cup of tea
but Life's what you
      make it, eh?
O you must come and join me by the seaside!
Because we all like to be beside the

sea

The Unfairness Of Birds

(*a pantoum*)

Most birds are so unfair.
They'll eye you up and down
and leer and jeer like lager louts
and taunt you with their flying skills.

They'll eye you up and down,
they have no tact, they screech about,
and taunt you with their flying skills,
they clearly just don't care.

They have no tact, they screech about
how colourful their feathers are.
They clearly just don't care
for quieter things like reading.

How colourful their feathers are!
Why can't *we* be green and red and loud?
For quieter things like reading
though, one has to quell one's wilder side.

Why can't *we* be green and red and loud
and go on sorties, precision-bombing cars?
(Though one has to quell one's wilder side.)
In spring, they'll land on your head

(and go on sorties, precision-bombing cars).
They act as though they own the place
in spring. They'll land on your head,
and even your face, if they're in the mood.

They act as though they own the place,
then *holy crap* your windscreen's white.
And even your face if they're in the mood!
Those birds are so unfair.

66° 33' 47" N   180° 0' 1" W

6. A NEW UNIVERSE

Filaments

A thousand miles of open sea
                        settles, separates, holds us spellbound,
holds the filaments and chambers
                        of our provenance and our destiny,
troves of misplaced memories
                        that collectively roam
the coralline fields.

Horizonal clouds plump in the haunted yonder
                        like ellipses in search of brighter endings
(our edgeless world's curvature breaks
                        a straighter view),
while below the surface,
                        submarine trenches and forests of kelp disappoint
filum-boned hunters.

Staring down this wild expanse,
                        we clutch at the air, you and I, for a handhold
and dream up tenuous fibrils of linkage,
                        faithful venules, mere lines on a page,

like an architect's afterthought,
                        such as telephone wires and undersea cables
nestled in weed.

We're always listening for the sound of
                        optic fibres snapping to silence and
fractious satellites crashing to earth.
                        This fear of departure and loss,
this inkling of loneliness and failure
                        is a statued permanence
in our earthbound fix,

a plinth for our faithless times –
                        a constancy, like the heated tungsten
that kindles our moonless nights
                        spent in curtained rooms,
or the clusters of galaxies
                        that witness our cross-continental tears
and cast down false light.

All hope lies beyond the offing,

                as does despair.

The frigidity of distance

         may be its own reward, with faraway fiefdoms
insinuating a frozen appeal,

              yet longinquity alone with its unspannable
stretches and outposts

can never undo the cilium-thin craftiness of intent.

                    Thought is faster than light.

Somewhere beyond beaches you live a life

          corralled from mine, and beyond this universe
we are, theoretically, unacquainted, and yet

             our connection is an obdurate fact and it's only
the papery wall of theory

that lies between us.

The Orval

Five mobled Orpiments stood in wait,
ruddled in a puzzle of their own making,
when an Orval appeared, royning her arrows
and smiling ferreously.

The ceratoid circle of clowns leered diacidly,
their rubiginous grimaces masking their fear,
while their nemesis, taking her time,
simply riled her way by.

Halcyone's Tears

[Halcyone *is pronounced Hal*-SIGH-*oh-nee.* Ceyx *is* SEE-*iks.*]

>Halcyone's tears
>formed mirroring pools
>at her feet.
>
>The messenger Morpheus
>had left her to her
>sorrow: a thunderbolt
>
>cast in anger by the
>unspeakable Zeus
>had sunk Ceyx's ship
>
>and drowned him –
>Ceyx, her much
>loved husband.
>
>Halcyone made her
>way to the sea
>at midnight.
>
>A storm had tilted
>through and churned
>the black waters to

a foaming brew
of brine and weed
and fish – the tide

was overreaching. When
she walked with war-steps
into the raging surf and

offered her bare breasts
to Poseidon, she knew
she would die

but not that the gods
should pity them, not proud
Ceyx and Halcyone.

When their lifeless bodies
buoyed to the surface
of the now calm, gold-

speckled sea, Halcyone's
hair floated about
her devoted head like a halo

or the mane of a lion.
Ceyx's face held its rage,
even when their dead limbs

touched. And then,
in the flash of a godseye,
they were kingfishers,

divinely cast, flicking
the thick, mirroring
sheen of the landless sea,

together, and flying east,
into the sun, contented
as never before and free.

The Blue Beauty

While landing – descending over oblong fields,
(surrendering to gravity's compulsion,
and coaxing friction from the faithless air) –
you look up and out and see the Blue.

An alien unveiling; a spill of secrets,
like a flash of sapphire on a lonely beach:
tablecloth clouds reveal a splendour born
in a place beyond experience or dreams.

Above a blur of mangroves, you negotiate
the depths of this discovery. Of her.
A distant logic but a warm embrace, as light
as mist, as deep as five stacked seas.

The Blue is proof of beauty.
It cannot be taken, or tended, or touched.
It can only be glimpsed, or longed for.
It's always too much, and it's never enough.

Aphrodite Unnosed

Inspired by the sculpture L'Afrodite accovacciata, *or* Crouching Aphrodite
*(circa 250 BC, marble, 106cm) on display at the Museo Nazionale Romano,
Palazzo Massimo, Rome.*

You'll blink at the world
when you enter it
and rush to curves.

You'll entice sweet words
and make men weep,
you'll burn the heavens briefly white

and later, yes, you'll die.
But in that deepest
sleep your life

will flow to marble
in a Carrara-smooth rebirth
of the latest goddess.

Your snow-bright skin
will throb with life —
clothes-less, breath-less,

ineffably desired: your legs,
your cherished breasts,
your loins ablaze,

your perfect face... and also
them, they'll be there too,
helter-skelter right behind you,

those rowdy dogs of Ruin
with their love of rank Decay
and the quaking crush of History.

Your arms will go, and half
your head. You'll lose
your eye. And then your nose.

Unnosed, and soon to be unknown.
And then, at last, perhaps, the gods
will leave you to your dreams.

[] – Postscript

Discovery is the currency
of hidden meridians

where every dawn is a door
to a new universe

and every day is another life lived.

Littoral Motion

As terns fill the sky with their riotous turning
and gulls, with their wheeling and dealing and swoop,
as unflappable pelicans switch from gliding to sliding
and a solitary hawk quits a questioning loop,

as ghostly whiting whisper through sun-speckled shallows
and a jellyfish washes in, shyly, to shore,
as a fish with no tail arrives at my feet furious,
and to no avail flips and flops, and flip-flops some more,

I move along the flat damp sand, not walking but shifting,
between states, like the itinerant breeze or the shape of the sea,
because the beach and the clouds and the wind and the ocean
are highways just waiting for voyagers like me.

PREVIOUS PUBLICATIONS

Poems in this collection have previously appeared in the following publications:

Meanjin [*Augmented Sonnet For A Trophy Wife*; *A Closer Inspection* – Autumn 2016]
Southerly [*The Snow That Was Falling All Day* – February 2018]
Cordite [*The Einsteinian Qualities Of Distance* – May 2017]
Poetry Salzburg Review [*The Conquistador*; *The Longreach Desperado*; *Littoral Motion* – Summer 2016; *By The Lee Of The Bitter Wind*; *A Walk On The Glacier* – Spring 2018]
Manufactured (Hermes, 2015) [*The News*; *The Dog On The Log*]
Warped (Hermes 2016) [*Death Mask*; *Goldbricker*; *Modern Sex*]
Imprint (Sydney University Press, 2016) [*The Murder (Of Crows) – Country Circuit*; *Leaves And Dust*; *Lows And Highs*]
Return Ticket From Sydney To Bistrita (Australian-Romanian Academy Publishing, 2021) [*Sunrise*; *Lost Explorer, Beyond Hope, Reaches Mount Oblivion*].

www.markmacrossan.com

www.ingramcontent.com/pod-product-compliance
Lightning Source LLC
Chambersburg PA
CBHW020324010526
44107CB00054B/1970